FINANCIALLY SMART

CONTENTS

FINANCIALLY SMART
UNDERSTANDING YOUR MONEY

Welcome to the world of becoming financially smart! As a young adult, you are at an important stage in your life where you can start learning about managing your finances, wage taxes, investing and more . This workbook is designed to teach you the basics of finance and to help you get off to a solid financial future.

FINANCIALLY SMART
LEARNING ABOUT MONEY

CHAPTER 1

Money is an essential part of our lives, but many people struggle to understand it. In this chapter, we'll explore the basics of money, including what it is, how it works, and why it's important to understand. By the end of this chapter, you'll have a better understanding of money and its role in our lives.

What is Money?

Money is used to buy goods and services and is considered a medium exchange. It can take many forms, including paper bills, coins, and digital currency. Money is used to facilitate transactions between buyers and sellers, and it has been essential for thousands of years.

How Money Works

Money works through a system of trust and value. People trust that the money they receive is worth something because it is backed by a government or other entity that ensures its value. For example, the US dollar is backed by the US government, which means that people trust it as a medium of exchange.

Money also has value because it is limited. There is only a finite amount of money in circulation, which means that it has value because it is scarce. This is why governments and central banks control the money supply, to ensure that there is enough money in circulation to facilitate transactions but not so much that it loses its value.

FINANCIALLY SMART
LEARNING ABOUT MONEY

Understanding money is essential for making smart financial decisions. Here are a few reasons why:

Budgeting: Money management begins with understanding how much money you have and how much you need to spend. Without this understanding, it's difficult to create a budget and stick to it.

Investing: Investing your money is a way to grow your wealth over time, but it also comes with risks. Understanding how different types of investments work, such as stocks, bonds, and real estate, can help you make informed decisions and minimize your risks.

Debt Management: Many people struggle with debt, and understanding how interest rates and payments work can help you manage your debt more effectively and avoid falling into a cycle of debt.

Economic Decisions: Money plays a critical role in the economy, and understanding how the economy works can help you make informed decisions about things like buying a home, starting a business, or saving for retirement.

In summary, money is essential for making smart financial decisions related to budgeting, investing, debt management, and economic decisions.

FINANCIALLY SMART
BUDGETING

CHAPTER 2

Budgeting is a crucial part of personal finance that can help you achieve your financial goals and avoid debt. In this chapter, we'll discuss the basics of budgeting, including why it's important, how to create a budget, and some best practices to follow.

Why Budgeting is Important

Budgeting is important for several reasons. First, it helps you keep track of your income and expenses, so you can make sure you're living within your means. Second, it allows you to prioritize your spending and allocate your money towards the things that matter most to you. Finally, it can help you achieve your financial goals, such as saving for a down payment on a vehicle, paying off debt, or building an emergency fund.

How to Create a Budget

Creating a budget can seem overwhelming at first, but it's a straightforward process. Here are the steps you can follow to create a budget:

Determine your income: Calculate your monthly income, including your salary, any freelance or side hustle income, and any other sources of income.

FINANCIALLY SMART
BUDGETING

Track your expenses: Make a list of all your monthly expenses, including fixed expenses like rent or mortgage payments, car payments, and utilities, as well as variable expenses like groceries, entertainment, and dining out. Use a budgeting app or spreadsheet to make this easier. Categorize your expenses: Group your expenses into categories, such as housing, transportation, food, entertainment, and savings.

Set financial goals: Determine your financial goals, such as paying off debt or saving for a down payment on a vehicle.

Allocate your money: Allocate your money towards your various expenses and financial goals. Be sure to prioritize your essential expenses, such as housing and transportation, before allocating money towards discretionary expenses like entertainment.

BEST PRACTICES FOR BUDGETING

Be realistic: Don't set unrealistic goals or try to cut your spending too drastically. This will only make it harder to stick to your budget in the long run.

Review your budget regularly: Review your budget regularly to make sure you're staying on track. Adjust your budget as needed.

Build an emergency fund: Build an emergency fund to cover unexpected expenses. This will help prevent you from going into debt when something unexpected happens.

FINANCIALLY SMART
BUDGETING

Use cash or a debit card: Use cash or a debit card for your discretionary expenses, such as entertainment or dining out. This will help you avoid overspending.

Stay disciplined: Stick to your budget and stay disciplined, even when faced with temptations to overspend.

Budgeting is an essential part of personal finance that can help you achieve your financial goals and avoid debt. By understanding the importance of budgeting, how to create a budget, and best practices to follow, you can be on your way to financial success. Just remember to stay disciplined, stay realistic, and stay focused on your long-term goals.

FINANCIALLY SMART
BANKING

CHAPTER 3

Banking is a fundamental aspect of modern finance and a critical component of the global economy. In this chapter, we will explore the basics of banking, including its functions, types, and importance. By the end of this chapter, you will have a better understanding of banking and its role in the financial system.

FUNCTIONS OF BANKS

Banks provide a wide range of services, including:

Deposits: Banks accept deposits from individuals and businesses and pay interest on them. Deposits can be made in various forms, such as savings accounts, checking accounts, and certificates of deposit.

Lending: Banks provide loans to individuals and businesses for various purposes, such as buying a home, starting a business, or financing a car. Banks make a profit by charging interest on loans.

Payment Services: Banks provide payment services, such as issuing credit and debit cards, processing checks, and facilitating wire transfers.

Investment Services: Banks offer investment services, such as brokerage services, mutual funds, and retirement accounts.

TYPES OF BANKS

There are several types of banks, each with different functions and regulatory requirements.

FINANCIALLY SMART
BANKING

Commercial Banks: Commercial banks provide a wide range of services, including deposits, lending, and payment services, to individuals and businesses. They are typically the largest and most visible type of bank. Investment Banks: Investment banks specialize in providing investment services, such as underwriting securities and facilitating mergers and acquisitions.

Central Banks: Central banks are responsible for monetary policy and regulating the financial system. They also provide services to commercial banks, such as maintaining reserve requirements.
Online Banks: Online banks operate exclusively online and offer many of the same services as traditional banks.

IMPORTANCE OF BANKING
Banking is critical to the functioning of the global economy. Here are a few reasons why:

Facilitating Transactions: Banks provide a safe and efficient way for individuals and businesses to transfer money and make purchases. Promoting Economic Growth: By providing loans to individuals and businesses, banks help spur economic growth and job creation.

Ensuring Financial Stability: Banks play a critical role in maintaining the stability of the financial system. They are regulated to ensure that they maintain adequate capital reserves and follow sound lending practices. Providing Financial Services to the Underserved: Banks provide financial services to underserved communities, such as low-income individuals and rural areas, to promote financial inclusion.

FINANCIALLY SMART
BANKING

In summary, banking is a critical component of modern finance and the global economy. Banks provide a wide range of services, including deposits, lending, payment services, and investment services. There are different types of banks, each with different functions and regulatory requirements. The importance of banking lies in its ability to facilitate transactions, promote economic growth, ensure financial stability, and provide financial services to the underserved.

DIFFERENCES BETWEEN A BANK AND A CREDIT UNION

Banks and credit unions are both financial institutions that offer similar services, but there are some key differences between the two:

Ownership: Banks are owned by investors, while credit unions are owned by their members. Credit unions are not-for-profit organizations that are run by a board of directors elected by their members.

Membership: Banks are open to anyone who meets their requirements, while credit unions have membership restrictions. Credit union membership is often limited to specific groups of people, such as employees of a certain company, members of a particular community, or members of a certain profession.

Products and services: Both banks and credit unions offer similar financial products and services, such as checking and savings accounts, loans, and credit cards. However, credit unions may offer lower fees and better interest rates on loans and savings accounts due to their not-for-profit status.

FINANCIALLY SMART
BANKING

Fees: Banks may charge higher fees for services like ATM withdrawals, overdrafts, and monthly account maintenance. Credit unions, on the other hand, may charge lower fees or no fees at all.

Accessibility: Banks often have a larger presence with more branches and ATMs, making them more accessible. Credit unions may have fewer branches and ATMs, but they may offer surcharge-free access to a wider network of ATMs.

Insurance: Both banks and credit unions are insured by the government, but through different agencies. Banks are insured by the Federal Deposit Insurance Corporation (FDIC), while credit unions are insured by the National Credit Union Administration (NCUA).

FINANCIALLY SMART
CREDIT

CHAPTER 4

In this chapter, we'll learn about credit. We'll discuss what credit is, how it works, and how to build credit. We'll also talk about the dangers of debt, and how to avoid falling into debt traps.

Credit is a financial tool that can be both helpful and harmful. In this chapter, we'll explore the basics of credit, including how it works, how to build and maintain good credit, and some common pitfalls to avoid.

WHAT IS CREDIT?

Credit is the ability to borrow money or obtain goods or services with the promise to pay later. Credit can come in many forms, such as credit cards, personal loans, car loans, and mortgages.

HOW DOES CREDIT WORK?

When you borrow money or obtain goods or services on credit, you are entering into a legal agreement to repay the amount borrowed, plus interest and any fees. Your creditworthiness, or the likelihood that you will repay the debt, is determined by your credit score, which is calculated based on your credit history, income, and other factors.

HOW TO BUILD AND MAINTAIN GOOD CREDIT

Building and maintaining good credit is important for many reasons. Good credit can help you obtain loans, credit cards, and other financial products at lower interest rates, which can save you money over time. Here are some tips for building and maintaining good credit:

FINANCIALLY SMART
CREDIT

Pay your bills on time: Paying your bills on time is one of the most important things you can do to maintain good credit. Late payments can have a negative impact on your credit score.

Keep your credit utilization low: Credit utilization is the percentage of your available credit that you are using. Keeping your credit utilization below 30% can help you maintain good credit. **(download my free credit utilization app on the APP Store and Google Play)**

Monitor your credit report: Check your credit report regularly to make sure there are no errors or fraudulent activity. You are entitled to one free credit report per year from each of the three major credit bureaus.
Use credit responsibly: Only use credit when you need to, and make sure you can afford to repay the debt. Avoid maxing out your credit cards or taking on more debt than you can handle.

HERE ARE SOME COMMON CREDIT PITFALLS THAT YOU SHOULD AVOID:

- Late payments: One of the most common credit pitfalls is making late payments. Late payments can have a negative impact on your credit score, and they may also result in late fees and increased interest rates.
- Maxing out your credit cards: Another common mistake is maxing out your credit cards. When you use up all of your available credit, it can hurt your credit score and make it difficult to obtain new credit in the future.

FINANCIALLY SMART
CREDIT

- Applying for too many credit cards: Applying for too many credit cards at once can also damage your credit score. Each time you apply for credit, it results in a hard inquiry on your credit report, which can lower your score.
- Ignoring your credit report: Your credit report is an important tool that can help you manage your credit score. If you ignore it, you may miss errors or fraudulent activity that can hurt your credit.
- Co-signing a loan: Co-signing a loan for someone else may seem like a helpful gesture, but it can be risky. If the other person doesn't make their payments on time, it can damage your credit score.
- Closing old credit accounts: Closing old credit accounts can also hurt your credit score. When you close an account, it reduces your available credit and may shorten your credit history, which can lower your score.
- Failing to budget: Finally, failing to budget can make it difficult to manage your credit effectively. If you spend more than you can afford to pay back, it can result in missed payments and damage to your credit score.

By avoiding these common credit pitfalls, you can keep your credit score healthy and increase your chances of obtaining credit in the future.

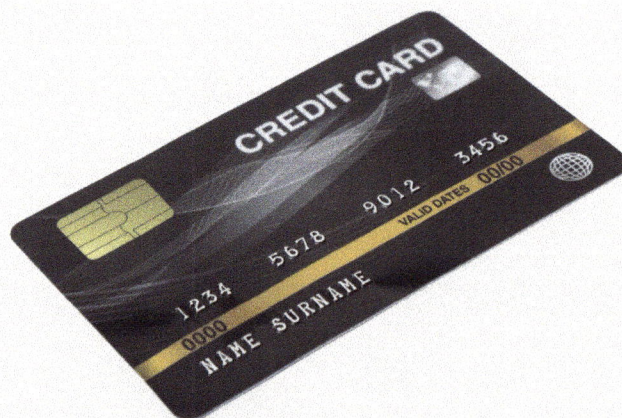

FINANCIALLY SMART
UNDERSTANDING WAGE TAXES

CHAPTER 5

Wage taxes refer to the amount of money that an employer deducts from an employee's paycheck to pay for the employee's income tax and other mandatory taxes. Wage taxes are essential for the proper functioning of any economy, as they fund various government programs and services. In this chapter, we will discuss the basics of wage taxes, including what they are, how they work, and how they affect employees and employers.

WHAT ARE WAGE TAXES?

Wage taxes are the taxes that are deducted from an employee's paycheck to pay for their income tax, Social Security tax, and Medicare tax. Income tax is the tax that employees pay on their income, and it is calculated based on their income and deductions. Social Security tax is a payroll tax that funds Social Security benefits, and Medicare tax is a payroll tax that funds Medicare.

HOW DO WAGE TAXES WORK?

Wage taxes are calculated based on an employee's gross pay, which is their total earnings before any deductions.

Employers are required by law to deduct the correct amount of wage taxes from their employees' paychecks and remit them to the appropriate government agencies. Employers are also responsible for paying their share of Social Security and Medicare taxes.

FINANCIALLY SMART
UNDERSTANDING WAGE TAXES

The amount of wage taxes an employee pays depends on their income level and their tax filing status. The more an employee earns, the higher their income tax rate. Additionally, employees who are married and file jointly or who have dependents may be eligible for certain deductions and credits that can reduce their tax liability.

HOW DO WAGE TAXES AFFECT EMPLOYEES?
Wage taxes have a significant impact on employees' take-home pay, as they reduce the amount of money that employees receive in their paychecks. However, employees can take steps to minimize the amount of wage taxes they pay, such as contributing to a 401(k)-retirement plan or claiming deductions and credits on their tax return.

HOW DO WAGE TAXES AFFECT EMPLOYERS?
Employers are responsible for withholding and remitting their employees' wage taxes, which can be a complex and time-consuming process. Employers may also be subject to penalties and fines if they fail to withhold or remit the correct amount of wage taxes. Additionally, employers are required to pay their share of Social Security and Medicare taxes, which can be a significant expense for businesses.

Understanding the basics of wage taxes is essential for both employees and employers, as it can help them comply with tax laws and regulations and make informed financial decisions.

FINANCIALLY SMART
RENT-TO-OWN

CHAPTER 6

You are moving into your first apartment and don't have a television, furniture or appliances. Since you paid your down payment and first month's rent, you are now low on cash. You come across an ad for a Rent-to-Own center and you see just $29.99 per week for 18 weeks and you think this may be the best way to get the items that you need. The thought of owning the merchandise at the end of the contract makes this process seem even more appealing. Over the last few years, you heard a few horror stories from family members who used this service and you are not sure whether or not you should take this route. There are a few things you should know before deciding whether or not to go ahead with this option.

Rent-to-Own companies will advertise in such an attractive way, that it seems like the best option by stating things like, "you will own your purchase in as little as 18 months" or "no credit, no problem" but buyer beware! These plans are pleasing to people who may have bad credit or limited cash. People who use this type of program often fail to realize that by the end of the contract, you often will have paid two to three times the suggested manufacturers retail price.

HERE'S AN EXAMPLE:

Rodney's television breaks down. The Super Bowl is coming up in four months and he doesn't have the cash or credit card to purchase a new one. He comes across an advertisement that reads, "You can own this big screen television, no money down, for just $40.00 per week for 48 weeks." The manufacturers suggested retail price on this television is $650. This sounds great to Rodney because he is not sure how he can get a new one in time for the game.

FINANCIALLY SMART
RENT-TO-OWN

What Rodney failed to realize is how much he will end up paying by the end of the contract. By the time he is at the end of his contract, the price paid for the television minus sales tax and other applicable fees will amount to $1,920. He could have purchased three televisions for this price.

The questions you need to ask yourself before agreeing to a rent-to-own contract are:
- What happens if I miss a payment?
- How long is the contract?
- When are my payments due?
- Who will pay for repairs if the merchandise breaks down before the contract ends?

Rent-to-Own programs may be a good idea if you want to try merchandise before you buy it or if you just need it for short period of time. If you plan on renting long-term or if you want to just purchase, then "Buyer Beware" with this type of program.

There are a few other alternatives, if you decide this option isn't the best one for your. Here are a few suggestions:
- Consider purchasing used merchandise that could save you a lot of money.
- Buy used furniture from second-hand furniture stores or seek out garage sales
- Start a savings for the merchandise that you want to purchase.
- Check with retailers to see if they offer In-House financing, what the terms are and if you would qualify.

FINANCIALLY SMART

RENT-TO-OWN: BUYER BEWARE (EXERCISE)

- Borrow a personal loan if not from a bank then from family or a friend. Caution! Sometimes borrowing from family and friends can lead to personal issues and uncomfortable relationships.
- If you have a credit card with a low limit, consider requesting a higher limit to purchase. Contact your credit card company to see if this is possible. Most times this can be done without impacting your credit.

1. Crystal's refrigerator stops running and she doesn't have a credit card with a limit high enough to purchase a new one. She is in the process of rebuilding her credit. Her local rent-to-own store is running an ad in the newspaper for full-sized refrigerator without a credit check or down payment. The payment plan is $99.00 a week for 18 weeks. Below that advertisement was one featuring a new refrigerator on sale for $900.00 at her local appliance store. Minus fees, how much will Crystal end up paying at the end of her contract?

Answer: _____

Other Alternatives that Crystal can possibly explore: _____

_____

FINANCIALLY SMART
RENT-TO-OWN: BUYER BEWARE (EXERCISE)

2. Dan and Keisha are moving into a new house in 90 days. Their new home already has a washer and dryer. In their old house, that they are still living in, their washer and dryer both stopped working. Keisha seen an advertisement for a washer/dryer combo for $30 per week for 35 weeks, no long-term commitment. Is a rent-to-own contract a good idea for Dan and Keisha?

Answer: _____

If yes, why? _____ If no, why not?_____

ANSWER KEY

1.$1,782.00
Crystal can request a credit limit increase. Crystal can alos purchase a used refrigerator until she save enough funds for a new one.

2. Yes
Yes, a rent-to-own contract would be a good idea for Dan and Keisha because they would just need to temporarily rent for 90 days. There are no long-term commitments.

FINANCIALLY SMART
INVESTING

CHAPTER 7

In this chapter, we'll teach you about investing. We'll discuss the different types of investments, such as stocks, bonds, and mutual funds. We'll also talk about the benefits of investing early, and how to start investing with a small amount of money.

Investing is an important aspect of personal finance that can help you build wealth and achieve your long-term financial goals. In this chapter, we'll discuss the basics of investing, including the different types of investments, how to start investing, and some best practices to follow.

TYPES OF INVESTMENTS

There are many different types of investments, each with their own level of risk and potential reward. Some common types of investments include:

Stocks: Stocks represent ownership in a company and can be bought and sold on stock exchanges.

Bonds: Bonds represent debt issued by companies or governments and typically pay a fixed interest rate.

Mutual funds: Mutual funds are a type of investment that pools (two or more organizations or people putting money into a common fund) money from multiple investors to buy a diversified portfolio of stocks, bonds, or other assets.

FINANCIALLY SMART
INVESTING

Exchange-traded funds (ETFs): ETFs are like mutual funds, but they trade like stocks on an exchange.

Real estate: Real estate investments can include rental properties, REITs (real estate investment trusts), and real estate mutual funds or ETFs.

HOW TO START INVESTING

Before you start investing, it's important to have a solid understanding of your financial situation, including your income, expenses, and debt. You should also have an emergency fund in place to cover unexpected expenses.

Once you're ready to start investing, here are some steps you can follow:

Determine your investment goals: What are you investing for? Are you saving for retirement, a down payment on a house, or something else?

Choose your investments: Based on your goals and risk tolerance, choose the types of investments that are right for you.

Open an investment account: You can open an investment account with a brokerage firm or through your bank.

Fund your account: Deposit money into your investment account to start investing.

FINANCIALLY SMART
INVESTING

Monitor your investments: Keep track of your investments and adjust as needed.

BEST PRACTICES FOR INVESTING

Here are some best practices to follow when investing:

Diversify your portfolio: Don't put all your money into one type of investment. Instead, spread your money across different types of investments to reduce risk.

Invest for the long-term: Investing is a long-term game. Don't get caught up in short-term fluctuations in the market.

Keep fees low: Be mindful of fees associated with your investments, such as brokerage fees and management fees.

Rebalance your portfolio: Over time, your investments may become unbalanced. Rebalance your portfolio periodically to maintain the appropriate mix of investments.

Investing is an important part of personal finance that can help you build wealth and achieve your financial goals. By understanding the different types of investments, how to start investing, and best practices to follow, you can be on your way to a successful investing journey. Just remember to stay patient, stay informed, and stay focused on your long-term goals.

FINANCIALLY SMART
PURCHASING A VEHICLE

CHAPTER 8

Purchasing a vehicle can be a significant investment, both financially and personally. Whether you're buying your first car, upgrading to a newer model, or adding a vehicle to your collection, there are several factors to consider before making a purchase.

The following chapter will guide you through the key steps involved in purchasing a vehicle, from setting a budget to negotiating the sale.

DETERMINE YOUR BUDGET

Before you start shopping for a vehicle, it's essential to determine your budget. Your budget should consider the total cost of owning a car, including the purchase price, insurance, fuel, maintenance, and repairs. Consider your current income, expenses, and financial goals to determine how much you can afford to spend on a vehicle.

RESEARCH YOUR OPTIONS

Once you have a budget in mind, research the types of vehicles that fit within your price range. Look for cars that meet your needs, such as fuel efficiency, cargo capacity, and safety features. Read online reviews and compare models to narrow down your options.

TEST DRIVE VEHICLES

When you have a list of potential cars, test drive them to get a feel for how they handle and how comfortable they are. Make sure the car meets your needs and is a good fit for you and your lifestyle. Take your time during the test drive and don't hesitate to ask questions or request additional information.

FINANCIALLY SMART
PURCHASING A VEHICLE

CHECK VEHICLE HISTORY REPORTS

Before making an offer, it's important to check the vehicle's history report. This report will reveal any accidents, previous owners, and any other issues that the car may have had. You can obtain a vehicle history report online, and it's a good idea to do this for any car you are seriously considering.

NEGOTIATE THE SALE

Once you have found a car you like, negotiate the sale with the seller. Be prepared to walk away if the seller isn't willing to meet your terms. Consider factors like the car's condition, age, mileage, and any repairs or upgrades that may be needed. Negotiate a fair price for both parties, and make sure that all terms are included in a written contract.

ARRANGE FINANCING

If you require financing, arrange this before making the final purchase. Shop around for the best interest rates and loan terms and compare offers from multiple lenders. Be sure to read the fine print and ask any questions before agreeing to a loan.

FINALIZE THE PURCHASE

When you have agreed on a price and arranged financing, finalize the purchase. Make sure to get all the necessary paperwork, including a bill of sale and registration documents. Pay for the car with a certified check or cash and take possession of the vehicle.

Purchasing a vehicle requires careful consideration of your budget, research, and negotiation skills.

FINANCIALLY SMART
PURCHASING A USED VEHICLE

Purchasing your first vehicle is a huge, financial commitment. Purchasing a used vehicle can be even more of a financial commitment especially if there are major issues that come along with it. There are things you should look out for and questions you should ask before making such a commitment.

- What year is the vehicle?
- Is financing available?
- Was this vehicle ever in any accidents?
- How are the brakes and when were they last checked or replaced?
- How much mileage is on the vehicle?
- How many previous owners were there?
- Is the vehicle being sold "As Is" or under warranty?
- How old are the tires?
- Are there any mechanical problems?
- Is there any damage to the exterior or interior?
- Is a vehicle history report available?
- Do maintenance records exist and if so, where are they?
- What has been recently replace or repaired?

FINANCIALLY SMART
AUTO INSURANCE

CHAPTER 9

Auto insurance is an essential financial protection for drivers. In the event of an accident, it can cover the cost of damages, medical expenses, and liability claims. However, understanding the different types of coverage and how they work can be confusing. In this chapter, we will explore the basics of auto insurance and how to choose the right policy.

TYPES OF AUTO INSURANCE COVERAGE

There are several types of auto insurance coverage, each of which provides different types of protection. The following are the most common types of coverage:

Liability coverage: This type of coverage pays for damages and injuries you cause to other drivers or property in an accident. It is mandatory in most states and typically has two components: bodily injury liability and property damage liability.

Collision coverage: This type of coverage pays for damage to your vehicle in the event of a collision with another vehicle or object, regardless of who is at fault.

Comprehensive coverage: This type of coverage pays for damage to your vehicle caused by non-collision events such as theft, vandalism, fire, or natural disasters.

Personal injury protection (PIP): This type of coverage pays for medical expenses and lost wages for you and your passengers if you are injured in an accident, regardless of who is at fault.

FINANCIALLY SMART
AUTO INSURANCE

Uninsured/underinsured motorist coverage: This type of coverage pays for damages and injuries if you are in an accident with a driver who is either uninsured or has insufficient insurance to cover the damages.

CHOOSING THE RIGHT AUTO INSURANCE POLICY

When choosing an auto insurance policy, it is important to consider several factors, including:

Coverage limits: The coverage limits determine the maximum amount your insurance company will pay for damages or injuries in an accident. Higher coverage limits mean higher premiums, but also provide greater financial protection.

Deductible: The deductible is the amount you must pay out of pocket before your insurance coverage kicks in. A higher deductible can lower your premium but also increases your out-of-pocket expenses in the event of an accident.

Discounts: Many insurance companies offer discounts for good driving records, multiple policies, and safety features on your vehicle. Reputation and customer service: It is essential to choose an insurance company with a good reputation and excellent customer service, so you can rely on them when you need to file a claim.

FINANCIALLY SMART
AUTO INSURANCE

Auto insurance is a necessary expense for anyone who owns or operates a vehicle. It provides financial protection in the event of an accident, and choosing the right coverage can help you avoid significant financial losses. By understanding the different types of coverage, considering your needs and budget, and choosing a reputable insurance company, you can find the right auto insurance policy to meet your needs.

FINANCIALLY SMART
PAYDAY LOANS

CHAPTER 10

Payday Loans: A High-Interest Solution for Short-Term Financial Needs
In today's fast-paced world, many people find themselves struggling to make ends meet from paycheck to paycheck. When emergencies arise, such as unexpected medical expenses or car repairs, some individuals turn to payday loans as a solution to their financial woes. However, these loans come with high interest rates and fees that can quickly add up and lead to further financial struggles.

WHAT ARE PAYDAY LOANS?

Payday loans, also known as cash advances, are short-term loans that typically range from $100 to $1,000. These loans are typically due on the borrower's next payday, which is usually within two weeks. To receive a payday loan, the borrower must provide proof of income, a checking account, and a valid ID.

The interest rates for payday loans are extremely high, often ranging from 300 to 400 percent or more, depending on the lender and the state in which the borrower lives. Additionally, many lenders charge fees for loan processing, late payments, and other services. These fees can add up quickly and make the loan even more expensive.

WHY DO PEOPLE TAKE OUT PAYDAY LOANS?

There are many reasons why someone might consider taking out a payday loan. For many people, a payday loan is a quick and easy way to get cash when they need it most. These loans are often marketed to individuals who have poor credit or who cannot qualify for traditional bank loans.

FINANCIALLY SMART
PAYDAY LOANS

Payday loans can also be used to cover unexpected expenses, such as medical bills, car repairs, or home repairs. Many people also use payday loans to cover basic living expenses, such as rent or groceries, when they are short on cash.

THE RISKS OF PAYDAY LOANS

Despite their convenience, payday loans come with significant risks. The high interest rates and fees associated with these loans can quickly add up, making it difficult for borrowers to pay them off on time. When a borrower is unable to repay the loan, the lender may offer to extend the loan for an additional fee, which only adds to the cost.

This cycle of borrowing and extending loans can quickly lead to a cycle of debt, where borrowers are unable to pay off their loans and are forced to take out additional loans just to make ends meet. In some cases, borrowers may even be forced to declare bankruptcy.

ALTERNATIVES TO PAYDAY LOANS

If you find yourself in need of cash to cover unexpected expenses, there are several alternatives to payday loans that you may want to consider. These include:

Personal loans: Personal loans are available from banks and other financial institutions. While these loans may have higher interest rates than traditional loans, they are often much less expensive than payday loans.

FINANCIALLY SMART
PAYDAY LOANS

Credit counseling: Credit counseling services can help you develop a budget and manage your finances. They may also be able to negotiate with creditors to lower your interest rates and monthly payments.

Cash advances from credit cards: If you have a credit card, you may be able to get a cash advance. While this option can be expensive, it is often less expensive than payday loans.

Borrowing from friends or family: If you have a trusted friend or family member who can lend you money, this may be a better option than a payday loan.

In conclusion, payday loans can provide a quick and easy solution for short-term financial needs, but they come with significant risks. The high interest rates and fees associated with these loans can quickly add up, leading to a cycle of debt that can be difficult to escape. If you find yourself in need of cash, consider alternative options such as personal loans, credit counseling, or borrowing from friends or family before turning to payday loans.

FINANCIALLY SMART
UNDERSTANDING YOUR MONEY

Congratulations! You now have a solid understanding of the basics of finance and are on your way to building a strong financial foundation. Remember, the key to success is to start early, stay informed, and practice good financial habits. Best of luck in your financial journey!

FINANCIALLY SMART
CREDIT BUREAUS & REPORTING AGENCIES

Here are a list of consumer reporting agencies that will eventually have your personal credit information on file such as your address, place of employment, credit reports and credits scores. A few of these companies are used to build employment profiles, renting, and banking information.

Experian (Credit, Mix)
P.O. Box 4500, Allen, TX 75013

Equifax Information Services, LLC (Credit, Mix)
P.O. Box 740256
Atlanta, GA 30374-0256

Transunion (Credit, Mix)
P.O. Box 2000
Chester, PA 19016

LexisNexis (Mix)
Consumer Center, P.O. Box 105108, Atlanta, Georgia, 30348-5108

Innovis (Credit)
PO Box 1640
Pittsburgh, PA 15230-1640

ChexSystems Inc. (Banking)
Attn: Consumer Relations
7805 Hudson Road, Suite 100
Woodbury, MN 55125